# OLD DOUGLAS & COALBU

## Including DOUGLAS WATER, RIGSIDE and GLE

*by*

James Hamilton

Highland cattle can still be seen in the grounds of Douglas Castle, and 'Jock', who died in 1915 aged 21 years, was considered enough of an attraction to warrant being featured on a postcard. The man standing next to him is Thomas Ireland.

First published in the United Kingdom, 2000,
by Stenlake Publishing, Ochiltree Sawmill, The Lade,
Ochiltree, Ayrshire, KA18 2NX
Telephone / Fax: 01290 423114

ISBN 1 84033 095 3



## ACKNOWLEDGEMENTS

Thanks to the late Bob Welsh of Douglas; the late Jimmie and John Hamilton of Coalburn; and Ben Morris of Rigside for assistance with information and photographs. Thanks also to W.A.C. Smith for permission to use the picture on page 19.

## FURTHER READING

The books listed below were used by the author during his research. None of them are available from Stenlake Publishing. Those interested in finding out more are advised to contact their local bookshop or reference library.

*Statistical Account of Scotland*, 1792.
*New Statistical Account*, 1841.
*Third Statistical Account*, 1960.
*Douglasdale: Its History and Traditions*, J. D. Hutchison and Dr G. MacFeat.
Copies of the *Coalburn Chronicles*, *Douglas Digest* and *Rigside Record* in Lanark Library.

Douglas viewed from the bridge over the Douglas Water which formed part of the right-of-way from Coalburn to the village. At the end of the nineteenth century miners walked the four miles over the moors from Douglas to Coalburn to work in the pits being developed there, with the pit lamps on their bunnets the only illumination in the hours of darkness. It was a very exposed path with little shelter from storms. At the time the inhabitants of Douglas were huddled together in the streets which surrounded Old St Bride's church. In the 1920s, however, Lanark County Council began to build council houses, and gradually most families moved up the hillside from the valley plain as more building took place to the south, especially after the end of the 1939-1945 war. Ironically the right-of-way that the miners walked along has been closed since 1988 to allow the extraction of coal by opencast mining.

# INTRODUCTION

The villages of Douglas, Coalburn, Douglas Water and Rigside form a triangle, located within five miles of each other and situated near the M74. They are in the upper ward of Lanarkshire and are under the administration of South Lanarkshire Council.

The settlements were all producing coal in the years of deep mining, and all of them have had to face – or will have to face – the extraction of coal by opencast workings. This started in Coalburn in 1988 when Dalquhandy, the largest such working in Europe, went into production. It was followed by smaller schemes at Rigside and Douglas Water. Lately discussions have been taking place about opening another major opencast at Glespin. The extraction of coal by surface working has proved very controversial. Those who object to it complain about the nearness of the operations to their homes, the dust which ensues, the noise of heavy earth-moving vehicles and the disruption on the roads when the coal is taken away in heavy lorries. Those in favour point out that deep mining was very dangerous and unhealthy for colliers and this modern method at least brings some local employment, although admittedly not in the numbers of the years of deep mining.

Douglas is the only one of the villages that has a well-chronicled past. It still retains the maze of narrow streets around Old St Bride's Church that first began to appear over a thousand years ago. For centuries the life of the village was bound up with the noble family of Douglas, their castle, and the Cameronian Regiment. Until the coming of deep mining, Douglas's economy was based on agriculture and handloom weaving, with many people employed on the extensive estates administered from Douglas Castle.

Just over a mile from Douglas was Douglas West, a small mining village that was established in the 1890s and survived for seventy years. It was the old type of mining village, with homes for incoming workers built around the pit head; a model that was apt to isolate families from the wider community. Only a few houses are still inhabited, and a visitor today would never imagine that there were once rows of homes containing families, as well as a school, shops, miners' welfare institute and bowling green.

Glespin produced coal for centuries, but lost many families after the pits and mines ceased production in the 1960s. The village has suffered from an infrequent bus service, and no longer has a post office or any shops, with residents having to go to Douglas to uplift pensions, whilst depending on travelling vans for basic supplies.

The original Coalburn was a series of rows of houses built around pits in the mid-1800s. Over the years some consolidation has taken place, with building on the vacant ground between the rows, but Coalburn is still an elongated village that lies along the main thoroughfare. Coal has been extracted in and around the village for at least eight centuries, and its exploitation dates back to the establishment of the abbey at Lesmahagow or earlier. Apart from the opencast working of coal at Dalquhandy which is scheduled to finish extraction in 2003, there are no substantial employers in the area for men, who have to travel outwith the district to find work. The main employer for women in the district is the Auchlochan Trust which provides services for the elderly.

Rigside has been a coal-producing area for at least two hundred years. In the early 1990s it was presenting a run-down appearance because of a dwindling population (due to lack of local employment), but large sums of money have since been spent on modernising some early council houses, as well as building attractive new homes.

Douglas Water was a village of rows erected to house miners brought in to work Douglas Colliery when it opened in 1896. Men came from areas such as Glenbuck and Haywood where reserves were exhausted. Douglas Water lost its vitality when the rows were demolished and no replacement homes were built. As at Douglas West, the community-based welfare institute, bowling greens and tennis courts all ceased to function. Even the school has closed following the building of a new primary at Rigside in the 1990s. Former residents returning to the scenes of their childhood at Douglas Water are saddened at how this once happy village has been allowed to die.

There is no doubt that the extraction of coal in the villages has had an adverse effect on the environment, with some unsightly spoil heaps left and the land around the former collieries scarified. At least when opencast workings cease, efforts are made to rehabilitate the land, as evidenced at Coalburn.

Since the closing of the deep mines, Coalburn's population has dropped to less than half its previous level and now stands at 1,170; only 1,600 people live in Douglas. The figures for Rigside and Douglas Water are rather fluid at present because tenants have been decanted while some existing houses are modernised, and new homes that are being erected do not yet have their full quota of tenants.

Despite the unfortunate legacy of the industrial past, there are still beautiful surroundings for those living in the villages. When the opencast workings cease Coalburn will once again have open moors running towards the Poniel Burn, while the lovely wooded valleys of the River Nethan and Logan Water remain unspoilt to the west. The scenery along the road from the M74 to Douglas still has its charm, with its lochs and trees, and the folk of Douglas are blessed with unrestricted access to the former castle grounds. There is still the lovely glen between Douglas Water and Rigside, and those who like to walk can head for the open moorland leading to the Heacotes and Tinto Hill.

An early reference to the castle at Douglas appears in a chronicler's account of the confinement of a man there for implication in the murder of Duncan, Earl of Fife in 1288. In the succeeding centuries the castle was fought over and destroyed on at least four occasions in battles between the English and the Scots, as well as in local feuds among the Scottish nobility. Bonnie Prince Charlie stayed a day and a night at the castle on 23 December 1745 on his way north on a journey which culminated in his defeat at Culloden in 1746. With the exception of one tower (right background) which still stands today, the castle was completely destroyed by fire in 1758. The architect Robert Adam drew up plans for a very grand replacement, only part of which was ever built. In 1938 this was demolished, and Lanarkshire lost what would have been a major tourist attraction, and a great help to the deflated local economy following the closure of the collieries and mines.

'Castle Dangerous' (right), immortalised by Sir Walter Scott in the novel of the same name, is all that remains of the pre-1758 Douglas Castle. The grounds around the ruin are open to the public, and with three lakes, swans, and Highland cattle roaming among the parkland trees, are most attractive. The replacement castle designed by Robert Adam has gone, along with its stables, boathouse and fine gardens. The Douglas family, famous in Scottish history from the time of Robert the Bruce, married into the family of the Earl of Home which now administers the Douglas and Angus estates, as well as their lands in the Borders. The late earl, Alex Douglas-Home, had a distinguished career in politics, culminating in his being appointed Prime Minister.

The Gardener's Gate was made by a blacksmith who incorporated various shapes of garden implements into the framework. It was formerly in the grounds of Douglas Castle but is now preserved at Castlemains, a Lanarkshire residence of the Home family.

The vernacular houses (smaller picture) with their thatched roofs, lime-washed walls and small openings for doors and windows contrast markedly with the gatehouse of the Douglas estate, with its dressed stone and tiled roof. Note the infant being carried by its mother in a plaid held tightly to her body. The main picture shows the widened road and new wall that was built when the houses were demolished. The gatehouse still stands in 2000, and the gateway leads to the parklands of Douglas estate where pedestrians are allowed to wander.

Douglas Castle lodge, with its ornamental gateway, was built after Douglas station on the Lanark to Muirkirk railway line was opened. The imposing structure was designed to impress visitors arriving by train at the Earl of Home's castle. (In 1931 the station was renamed Happendon to avoid confusion with Douglas, Isle of Man.) The lodge was recently renovated prior to the opening of Cairn Lodge motorway services adjacent to it.

Part of Old St Bride's Church (right) is thought to date from the fourteenth century, although archaeologists are of the opinion that a church was in existence over a thousand years ago, and that the nucleus of the feudal village grew up around it. It was given the name of St Bride's (St Bridget's) after the patron saint of the Douglas family, and suffered damage at the time of the Reformation. In the 1600s part of the building was converted into the town jail and court house, although services were still held there until the new St Bride's Church (above) was built in 1781. About 1880, renovations to the old St Bride's by the 12th Earl of Home saved the building from complete ruin. The clock tower contains the oldest working clock in Scotland. This was reputedly given to the village by Mary Queen of Scots, and although this link has not been confirmed it has been proved that the clock was made during her lifetime. The old church contains the tombs of the Douglas Family, as well as flags belonging to the Lanarkshire Regiment of Militia, later the Lanarkshire 3rd and 4th Battalions of the Cameronians (Scottish Rifles).

The new St Bride's was built because the old church had become ruinous, and didn't have sufficient seating to accommodate the increasing number of families in Douglas. It was constructed in the plainest possible style at a cost of £500, and originally had a steeple. Unfortunately, at the time of its erection little respect was given to preserving old buildings, and much of the stone from the old St Bride's was purloined for the new church. In the mid-1800s absence from church was unknown, and in 1836 the parish minister reported that 'a hundred heads of families were waiting to get pews of their own'. In line with other churches in Scotland, St Bride's now has a diminishing congregation, and liberal space for anyone wishing to attend the Sunday services.

The single-storey cottage adjacent to the whitewashed house was the home of James Gavin, a local Covenanter who was a tailor to trade. During the religious disturbances of the 1600s, Gavin was involved in holding open-air services known as conventicles. He hid in a cave at the side of the Earnsalloch Burn to avoid arrest, but was found by Redcoats (Government forces), and arrested. Gavin subsequently placed a commemorative stone above the door of his house, bearing the wording: 'Here dwelt JAMES GAVIN, Tailor, a Hero of the Covenant. He incurred the special enmity of Claverhouse who wantonly severed the ears from his head with his own shears about the year 1684. To commemorate and perpetuate this brutal outrage, Gavin carved this stone with his own hand to put above the door of the house erected by him years after his return from banishment in the ISLAND of BARBADOES (*sic.*)'. Following the demolition of Gavin's house in recent years, the wording on the stone was carved on a new plaque which was incorporated in a cairn in a small memorial garden in the Main Street of Douglas.

There was a period of prosperity in Douglas *c.*1700 during which several new houses were built, one of which later became the Cross Keys Inn. The most notable feature within the house is an elaborately carved panel bearing a date, two sets of initials, and a coat of arms. The authors of *Douglasdale: Its History and Traditions* state that: 'The history attached to the design is a romantic one. In those days a lady of rank who took as her husband a man who was socially her inferior was regarded as having committed an unpardonable offence. Such a lady was Catherine Cranstoun. A member of a titled Scottish family, she had been residing in France for several years when she startled the fashionable world by eloping with her coachman. The couple fled to Scotland and as Catherine by her action forfeited her inheritance, they settled down to live a quiet life in Douglas in a position suited to their by no means affluent circumstances. The letters C.C. and N.V. carved above the fireplace are their initials and the coat of arms . . . is that of the Cranstoun family'. The oldest surviving house in the village, dating from 1621, stands opposite Old St Bride's. In its time it has served as a court house and prison, and was the Sun Inn for a period.

For centuries, until the centre of population moved from the ancient part of Douglas to the new housing estates off Springhill Road and Addison Drive, Townhead was the 'tap o' the toon'. The long-established Douglas Arms Hotel has catered for travellers since coaching days. The road from Edinburgh to Ayr, which passes through Townhead, was first made passable around 1773 but would be considered woefully inadequate by modern standards. Stones of all shapes and sizes were thrown unbroken on to it to be settled by passing carts, with the result that it was soon full of deep ruts. When turnpike roads were introduced the turnpike trusts, so bitterly resented at first, improved the surface of the roads, funding the work with money gathered from tolls. County councils introduced tarmacadaming around 1920.

This shop, a combined butcher's and grocer's, was run by John Weir and Son, and prior to that by John's father William Weir. The premises were let to Frank Graham for a period until the mid-1930s, after which Mr Graham moved to another shop in the Main Street. The old shop was then demolished to make way for a new butcher's and drapery for Douglas Co-operative Society.

Like many other villages in Lanarkshire, Douglas was short of homes for families after the end of the 1914-1918 war and the Government authorised the building of local authority housing, such as the developments at Kilncroft Terrace and Welldale Street. Behind the Baby Austin car (which has an early Motherwell registration number) stand wooden houses which were erected in the 1920s to provide temporary accommodation until brick houses could be built. These were still occupied at the end of the 1939-1945 war. In the late 1940s and over the next two decades additional council houses and an industrial estate were built to the south of old Douglas.

The upper picture, dating from around 1900, shows the sanatorium and cottage hospital at Douglas, which were gifted to the village by Lady Home of Douglas Castle. The cottage hospital was dependant on voluntary funds until 1948 when the National Health Service took financial responsibility for all medical care. For over a hundred years it has served Douglas and the surrounding villages, providing medical care for those who have been hospitalised, plus respite for those who look after the ill. When the sanatorium was no longer needed, part of the wooden structure was conveyed on a system of rollers by the committee of Douglasdale junior football team and erected as a pavilion at their ground, Crabtree Park. Another section of the building (lower picture) was transferred to the West End at Douglas to serve as a house. It has now been replaced by a cottage.

THE BUNGALOW, DOUGLAS. N.B.

St Bride's Quoiting Club were winners of the Lanarkshire Cup and the Scottish Consolation Cup in 1908. Quoiting was a popular sport, especially among the mining fraternity, possibly because little outlay was required to make a quoiting green. All that was needed was a flat piece of ground, a supply of clay, two marking pins and quoits. As well as games among friends, competitions with money prizes were held and spectators arranged bets among themselves on who would win. Douglas also had various football teams over the years, and for many seasons the local team, Douglasdale, played in the Lanarkshire Junior League with moderate success. In 1970 a team from Douglas won the Scottish Amateur Cup. Before 1900, a juvenile team from Glespin won the Hozier Cup. A curling club was established at Douglas in 1792, playing games against neighbouring villages during frosty weather. Douglas had a nine hole golf course, but this closed in the 1930s. The bowling club has a long history, and carpet bowls at halls in Douglas have also proved popular for decades.

The annual camp of the Lanarkshire Imperial Yeomanry was a colourful sight to be seen in the area around Douglas at the beginning of the twentieth century. The camp was often held in a field at the side of the road leading from Douglas to Douglas West, convenient for the shooting range there. Volunteers had always come forward to protect Britain when danger threatened – during the Second World War, for example, recruits rushed to join the Local Defence Volunteers, later renamed the Home Guard. Men joined the yeomanry for the opportunity to train and keep fit in the open air, as well to ride and work with horses. For many it was the only opportunity to have a week away from home in the summer, as holidays were beyond the purse of the working man.

Members of the Lanarkshire Imperial Yeomanry in the stables at camp in Douglas. Asides from the Yeomanry, Douglas has much older military connections. On 14 May 1689, at a time of unease in Scotland, a body of enthusiasts enrolled to support the new ruler, King William. As the men mainly came from the Douglas estates, they were known at first as the Angus Regiment after the Earl of Angus, a son of the Marquis of Douglas. The name was later changed to the Cameronian Regiment, in memory of a leading Presbyterian and Covenanter, Richard Cameron. After being incorporated into the British Army, the Cameronians built up an impressive history of service all over the world, although the regiment was disbanded following reorganisation within the army. A ceremony took place near the site of Douglas Castle on 14 May 1968 to mark this. A statue to the Earl of Angus by Thomas Brock stands at the top of the Craig Brae and the figure's outstretched hand points towards the field on the other side of the river where the regiment was originally enrolled.

The village of Douglas West, situated just over a mile from the centre of Douglas, was established just before 1900 and had virtually vanished by the 1960s. When the colliery was established at Douglas West, Castle Terrace (comprising 95 houses) and Douglas View Terrace (12 houses) were built to house the workers, along with better-quality homes for the colliery manager, under-manager, cashier, chief engineer and chief electrician. Some blocks of council houses were erected later. The Miners' Commission provided a welfare institute and bowling green, Douglas Co-operative Society opened a branch in the village, and a primary school was built there, so that the community, despite being isolated, was self-sufficient. Former residents like to reminisce about their happy times there. However, coal seams are not inexhaustible, and as reserves started to run out and conditions in the miners' rows failed to measure up to what families expected, it was decided to condemn the rows. No rebuilding took place at Douglas West, and replacement houses were erected at Douglas. All that remains of Douglas West today are a few isolated houses and the former school, now used as an outdoor centre by a Christian fellowship. When the colliery was closed, the surrounding land was left scarred, with spoil heaps littering the countryside where formerly there had been open moorland.

When the railway line from Lanark to Muirkirk was proposed, the Earl of Home refused to allow the line to traverse his land within sight of the castle, and the route was constructed over the horizon from his home, beyond a forest. This meant that Douglas didn't have a station in the village, and residents wishing to travel by train had to make their way to Douglas West (above) or Happendon. Douglas West station became a Mecca for people needing to travel to Lanark for work or for classes at the academy there. Many will tell of the rush to Douglas West on foot or by cycle to board an early morning train before buses began a feeder service from Douglas to the station in the 1930s. The railway at Douglas West was also used to transport coal from Douglas Castle Colliery to Lanark and beyond. On 5 October 1964 the stations at Muirkirk, Inches, Douglas West, Happendon, Ponfeigh, Sandilands and Lanark Race Course closed.

The village of Glespin lies in Douglas parish about three miles west of Douglas on the A70 road to Muirkirk. The area around the village has been associated with coal mining since at least 1790, when records show that good-quality coal was being extracted. In 1855 a pit at the junction of the Glentaggart and Glespin Burns was producing coal using an early system of deep mining. Two shafts were used, with the miners descending to the underground workings by long ladders down one, and the other used to pump water out and hoist the coal to the surface using an old-fashioned crank engine. This method of getting the coal to the surface was a tremendous step forward; hitherto women and children had carried it up the ladders on their backs. Water was always a problem in the mines and pits around Glespin, as there are several burns acting as tributaries to the Douglas Water in the vicinity. In 1934 John Robb lost his life in a mine when water rushed in. (His brother Tom had been crushed to death by a roof fall a few years earlier in a pit at Coalburn.) In 1943 three miners – William Clark, his son Victor and nephew John Reid – lost their lives when trapped by an inrush of water. At one time there were 34 mines working in the Glespin area. Boring has revealed tremendous untapped seams of coal, and proposals for the extraction of this coal by opencast are being debated at present. The upper photograph shows Wull Thorburn repairing a rail on the tip for the coal dirt adjoining the pithead at Carmacoup around 1940.

Since the closure of the mines and pits around Glespin about 1960, the population of the village has shrunk because of its isolation, the lack of opportunities for work within easy travelling distance, and the infrequency of the bus service. Glespin does not have a post office or shop, so its residents have to rely on travelling vans for basic necessities. Fortunately one local firm, Ramage Distribution, has built up a substantial business and provides local employment. South Lanarkshire Council is continuing the work of previous councils in refurbishing their stock of houses in rural areas such as Glespin, and has opened a new community hall to replace the former miners' welfare club (lower picture).

Coalburn originated as a collection of rows of houses at Coalburn, Braehead, Bellfield, Bankend (or Brockley) and Auchenbegg, mainly built around the pits and lime quarries that were being opened around 1850. Over the past 150 years the spaces between the rows at Auchlochan collieries, Braehead and Bellfield have been filled with private and council housing, to create the village of Coalburn. This photograph, taken from Braehead Farm (now the site of Bernard's Sawmill), shows the gates and signal box at Coalburn railway station. The shop on the right of the brig (demolished in the 1980s) bears the name 'Auchenheath Provident Co-operative Society' above the window; the society must have used the premises after Mackenzie built the shop and before the McGill family took over. In the 1920s, when the population was more than double what it is now, Coalburn had three co-operative societies: Coalburn and District; Abbeygreen; and Auchenheath. None of the three societies exist any more. The brig crosses the Coal Burn (more often referred to as the Black Burn) which gives its name to the village and is first noted on the Blaeu map of around 1600. The road in front of the house attached to the shop had to be raised when the brig was built in place of the ford formerly in use.

This picture, dating from *c.*1915, shows Braehead, one of the parts of the village where families first built cottages because of its proximity to the post office and railway station. Before the arrival of a bus service to Coalburn in 1924, the railway was particularly important. Mount View, near the top of the post office brae on the right, was built by the Arneil family, entrepreneurs in coal mining who sunk the Poniel Pit. The railway line in the foreground led from Coalburn station to the turning point at Bankend. On the left is the Station Hotel (demolished), with the building known for five decades as Auchenheath Co-operative Store on the extreme right (this has lain empty for years).

Coalburn post office was built over a hundred years ago by James Adam, son of the manager at the collieries at Bankend. This photograph was taken around 1910 when Adam also had a horse and carriage hiring business. The driver on the left is his nephew Jimmy Hamilton, who eventually inherited the business. Bob Boyd is holding the reins on the other carriage. James Adam also owned a stationer's shop, a butcher's shop which had a horse-drawn van that operated throughout the neighbourhood, and a slaughterhouse (situated across the road from the post office). His nephew Jimmy continued this comprehensive business, but specialised in the removal of livestock to and from Lanark market from local farms, as well as selling sacks of coal from a lorry. He also had a taxi hiring business and a petrol pump in the forecourt of the post office. (It seems ironic that in the 1930s, when there was no widespread car ownership in the village, Coalburn had four pumps selling petrol – at the post office, McGill's shop, Goldie's shop at Cairnhouse, and Naismith's garage. The village does not have a filling station in the 1990s.)

Bellfield School (upper picture) opened in 1876, closed on 31 January 1960, and was demolished soon afterwards. It replaced two small schools; one run by the community at Buchtknowes, the other by the coalmasters at Bankend. It taught pupils from the whole district, with some as young as five years old walking more than two miles to attend. Children were taught up to the age of 14, although many were exempted from attendance when they reached 13 and their absence from the family workforce could cause hardship in the home. In 1900 the school had a roll of over 500 pupils and space was so scarce that the play sheds had to be used as classrooms. The rows adjoining the school were known as Bellfield Rows, and were built for the Bellfield Collieries which stopped production in 1921. They had a life-span of around eighty years and were condemned and knocked down in the late 1920s because of the lack of basic facilities such as running water and flush toilets. Although living in overcrowded and primitive conditions, the families were rather reluctant to move into Coalburn's newly-erected council houses. The world Depression had set in and the heads of the households were either idle or on short time, making it difficult for them to pay the rent and rates for their new homes (which were much higher than in the rows). Coalburn School (lower picture), opened in 1908, was constructed to avoid pupils from the west side of the village having to walk over a mile to school, as well as to obviate the overcrowding at Bellfield school. From 1960 Coalburn took all the pupils of the district and became a primary school, with children from 11 to 16 years attending Lesmahagow High.

Being a scattered community, Coalburn held Sunday School services for children at Bankend, Braehead and Bellfield in the mid-1800s. Eventually the village population was sufficient for a mission station from Lesmahagow to be started, and not long afterwards, in 1893, a United Free Church was established. This thrived, and photographs survive showing over forty people in the church choir in the early 1900s. The original church (small picture) was destroyed by fire in 1918 and for a period services were held in the Victoria Hall. A replacement church was built and opened in 1922; the larger photograph shows the boys and girls of the Sunday School assembled around 1925 for their annual trip. The outings were to local farms and the children were conveyed in farmers' carts drawn by Clydesdale horses to enjoy milk and a bag of buns, as well as taking part in organised games and races. The Rev. Brian Cross took over the ministry in 1961 and on his retiral in 1998, Coalburn Church joined with Lesmahagow Old Parish Church, with the Rev. Sheila Mitchell taking over the ministry of both churches. Members of the Roman Catholic faith never had sufficient numbers to have a chapel in the village, but met to worship for some years in the Miners' Union Hall in Bellfield Road then later in the Silver Band Hall. It could not be said the hall was not ecumenical, for the Roman Catholics met on Sunday mornings and the Orange Lodge used the same premises on Sunday afternoons. Adherents of the Christian Brethren faith met in the Ebenezer Hall, and then its replacement, Elim Hall (now a builder's office).

A view of Tinto View Terrace (built in the 1890s and demolished around 1960) taken before the Victoria Hall was erected next to the white cottage in 1907. The terrace was a two-storey brick building of sixteen houses. Originally water was obtained from a pump, with shared wash-houses and dry closets at the rear of the building, although in the 1930s kitchenettes and inside water closets were installed. The houses were constructed for miners at one of the Bellfield Collieries, which was immediately adjacent to them. During the 1920s there was an old quarry not thirty yards from the houses which was used for upwards of fifteen years as the approved coup for household refuse for the whole village. Householders complained of rats running about the back doors, as well as the stench and fumes from smouldering ashes in the refuse dump. The fields opposite Tinto View Terrace are now the site of the wooden houses which form what is known locally as Timbertown. These were being built in 1939 when the Second World War broke out, and special permission was required to allow them to be completed. There are 104 wooden houses: 64 in Midfield Road, 12 in Beechmount Avenue and 28 in Bellfield Road.

Miners residing in Coalburn or Bankend Rows with ambitions to live in homes of better standards began to have dwellings built for their families around the 1890s. The transition from a single end in a miners' row to a cottage with its own piece of ground allowed households to grow their own vegetables, keep hens for eggs and to fatten a pig. Housewives could take pride in their more commodious homes, make jams and jellies from fruit grown in their own gardens, and often brewed wine from locally gathered fruit such as elderberries. The picture shows the following cottages from the left: Gall Cottage (stone for the walls came from the local quarry on the land of Mr Gall); Ivy Cottage; Daisylea; Sunnybrae; Avondale (the owner previously lived in Strathaven); Allandale (after the owners, the Allan family); Ingleside; with Tinto View Terrace beyond. Two cottages are still owned and tenanted by the original families.

The postcard bears the name of Coalburn Terrace, although these buildings (demolished around 1960) were renamed Pretoria Terrace after a battle in the South African War of 1899-1902. Pretoria Terrace was built of a bluish brick, and the two blocks were both two storeys high, with the lower houses entered from the front. The upper floor was reached by outdoor stairs at the rear, with short landings at the top. Water had to be carried up the stair from stand pumps and there was a jaw-box (sink) for disposal of waste water. Shared toilets and wash-houses were at the rear of the buildings. The terrace has been replaced by attractive terraced houses in a landscaped garden with addresses in Coalburn Road. (It was during the 1939-1945 war that streets and roads in Coalburn were named and each house given a number. Many quaint names for cottages and rows have since fallen into disuse.)

The Miners' Welfare Institute, now Coalburn Miners' Club, was opened on 3 July 1925 and consisted of a large hall with a stage upstairs, and a reading room, billiard room, lending library, and another room in which badminton was played downstairs. It replaced the 'reading room' housed in Coalburn Rows. Alcohol was not allowed on the premises. The institute was a happy meeting place for older men in the community who could converse and play dominoes, draughts or carpet bowls; the younger men played billiards, which was more popular at the time than snooker. The hall upstairs was used for socials, dances, and concerts etc., but its most popular function was as a cinema. With the arrival of television in the home and with fewer men employed in the pits, the institute had to change to survive, and a consensus of members agreed to convert the building into a club where alcohol was permitted. Profits from the club have been used to help finance the children's gala days (an annual event from 1925), old folk's treats etc. The two-storey building on the right was one of two blocks of sixteen houses that were known as Garden Street, and have since been demolished.

A photograph of the miners' rows at Bankend or Brockley dating from *c*.1900, with the Schooner pit in the distance. These rows were made up of 47 houses (16 with one apartment and 31 with two apartments), with Bankend Terrace a short distance away. The 'Wee Cottages' and Sawdust Row (4 houses of two-apartments, so-named because the walls were lined with sawdust for insulation) stood near the pit screening plant. Situated on bleak moors, collieries such as the Schooner were very exposed to the elements, and colliers were often soaked with rain going to and from their work. People often talk about 'the good old days', but in 1861 the hamlet had a population of 321, which means there would have been an average of six people to each house (the largest had merely two rooms). The Lanarkshire Medical Officer's 1909 report on Bankend noted that the houses had 'no damp course . . . roofs are not watertight . . . no gardens . . . no sinks . . . ashpits in broken-down condition', yet despite these observations it was another twenty years before the houses were condemned and the families rehoused in Coalburn so that the rows could be demolished. The remnants of the hamlet were obliterated during the opencast working of coal in the area in the 1990s.

Coalburn Rows were built for the Auchlochan pits numbered one to ten which were first operated by the Auchlochan Coal Company, then by William Dixon & Co. in the 1930s, and finally by the National Coal Board from 1947. One row had been demolished by 1924 but at that time there were still 30 houses occupied. These were 'tied' houses, and if a tenant left the company's employment or was sacked, the house had to be vacated. Electricity was brought to the village in the early 1930s, but the colliery company refused to pay for it to be supplied to their houses, nor would it permit tenants to have it installed at their own cost. After 1939, when the production of coal became vital to the war effort, the newly appointed Minister of Fuel ordered the company to provide electricity to the homes. Having been in service for around 100 years, the houses were razed in the 1950s. The council used the site to erect tenements known as 'the electric flats', so-called because they had electric under-floor heating. The two-storey building at the far end of the rows on the left was the original Coalburn Store, initially run by the coal company. It was subsequently run by various individuals including Jimmy Morris, Bobby Turner, John Lando, and Tom Wilson. After lying unused for a period, it was bulldozed in 1999 to make way for new housing.

Auchlochan No. 1 pit (in the background), known locally as 'The Maid', was at the height of production around 1907 when the author's father started work underground at the age 13 years and 3 months, having been given an exemption from attending school as the eldest of a family of eight. The bing from the pit was an eyesore in Coalburn for upwards of seventy years until it was removed during the first stages of the opencast working of coal in 1988. This area has now been landscaped and a path created from Gunsgreen to the Shoulderrigg right-of-way. The building in the centre is known as Coalburn Inns (always referred to in the plural) and has been supplying refreshment for at least 140 years. The original tenant was Nellie Cranstoun, and on the near side of the road (which leads to Middlemuir and Bankend) there was a reliable well, known as Nellie's Well, which provided water for the houses in the neighbourhood before Coalburn had a piped water supply. The upturned carts belonged to Chairlie Gordon Wilson. Chairlie was a busy contractor, who transported supplies from Coalburn station to the Dunside dams when the reservoir was being built, as well as delivering tons of coal to householders. The building on the extreme left was the ambulance shed where a horse-drawn ambulance was housed. It later held two motor ambulances belonging to the voluntary Coalburn Ambulance Association. The ambulances were taken over by the National Health Service in 1948 and removed to the centre at Motherwell.

Auchlochan Number Six Colliery. The Auchlochan collieries were major employers in the area, providing work for 270 men in 1894 and peaking at around 600 colliers in 1950. Thereafter there was a reduction in numbers as workable seams for deep mining ran out. Auchlochan Number Nine, the last colliery, closed in 1968.

Auchenbegg (the spelling varied over the years) is an area of Coalburn where coal was first extracted by surface mines. A colliery then operated for over 200 years before closing in 1922. The accompanying small row of houses and single detached dwelling were all condemned in the 1930s as unfit for habitation. John Harvie, a colliery worker with a small croft, lived in the cottage. One of his sons and two of his daughters were educated to become teachers, and all worked in local schools. An unusual feature of the colliery was that the bing was planted with trees, which came about because the laird at Stockbriggs who owned the colliery didn't want it to spoil the surroundings of his house. Every year those employed at the colliery had a sports day when in addition to all the usual sprints etc., competitions such as pillow fights, pitching pennies, climbing the greasy pole, and sack races were held. The picture shows Auchenbegg Colliery in 1900. In 1988 a new road was built joining Coalburn and Porterhall to allow opencast working to proceed at Auchenbegg and nearby Shoulderrigg.

Lime Row was situated on high ground in front of Coalburn Church and was tenanted for around 100 years until the 1950s. It was originally built for miners in the large lime quarries to the rear and a kiln was working nearby until 1890, but ceased production when cheaper supplies could be brought in from abroad. The row consisted of five houses, all of a single apartment except one. Nancy Prosser (née Bond) recently described living conditions at Lime Row in the 1940s: 'We had only yin room for ma faither, mither and me. There never wis running water in the hoose and we got oor supplies frae a pump at the beginning o' the raw. It wis a dry closet at the back o' the raw and nane o' the hooses had a back door so we had tae get tae the closets roon the end o' the raw. It wis nae fun goin' oot on a wet or snowy nicht. In really daurk nichts – there wis nae street lighting – we used ma faither's miner's carbide lamp to go roun' the back.' The author's maternal great-grandparents resided at Lime Row in 1861. Water was carried in pails into the homes from the pump while the barrels caught water for washing clothes.

Coalburn Rechabite Pipe and Drum Band was formed in 1894 when local men thrown idle for many months by a national miners' strike began to practise on chanters and with drum sticks. It prospered, and the members decided to make it a temperance band by annexing the name Rechabite to it. (In the early years members who broke the pledge were forced to leave.) By 1907 the band had built the Victoria Hall, where its members have practised ever since. In 1935 it was asked to lead 10,000 people in a march at Bellevue, Manchester, at the 100th anniversary of the founding of the Independent Order Of Rechabites. Blessed with willing helpers and a community that appreciates it, the services of the band continue to be in great demand. One noticeable change in recent decades is the number of girl pipers and drummers who now play in it. The photograph shows the band and office-bearers in 1950. *Back row:* Guy Whitefield; Donald Mathieson; Jock Cosgrove; Jock Dyet; Stewart Graham; Jock White. *Middle row:* Jimmy Findlay; Tam Findlay; Sam Clelland; Jimmie Hamilton; Guy Whitefield (senior); Wull Steele; Wull Clelland. *Front row:* J. Whitefield; Bruce Shaw; Tam Prentice; Willie Hair; Tam Hamilton; Bobby Greenshields.

In 1902 a letter sent to the *Hamilton Advertiser* invited persons living in Coalburn to a meeting with a view to forming a brass band. A nucleus of players, many of whom had learned to play instruments while serving in the Yeomanry, met and agreed to practise together, and thus the Coalburn Brass Band (later Coalburn Silver Band) was constituted. Like the Coalburn Rechabite Pipe Band, it was never sponsored by the local collieries, so was dependant on committees raising money for instruments, music and uniforms, and the committee members who have given so much of their time in the interests of the band over the years deserve great praise. The silver band committee knew that the prospects of survival would be enhanced by having a regular place to practise so voluntary workers converted three adjoining cottages into a band hall. In 1973 Coalburn Silver Band, having won the Scottish section, competed in the British championships at the Albert Hall in London. Today, Coalburn silver band is the only surviving town or village silver band in the administrative area of South Lanarkshire; this is surprising as hundreds of pupils at schools are now taught all types of musical instruments. The photograph shows the band after winning the Fourth Class Championship of Scotland in 1930. *Back row:* Jimmy Bryson; Dougie Bryson; Alex Hamilton; Willie Rankine; Willie Brown; Jimmy Walker; Arch. Brown; Bobby Walker; Dickie McLean. *Front row:* Davie Bradford; Jimmy Cornelius; John Cornelius; Jimmy ('Peem') Hamilton; Frank Cornelius (conductor); Jimmy Penman; Bobby Johnstone; Hugh White; Wull Bryson.

The Old Mill, Lintfield Bank, Coalburn.

The hamlet of Lintfieldbank lay about two miles east of Coalburn and had been in existence for over a hundred years before its tenants began to be rehoused in Coalburn from 1939 onwards. With the exception of one villa, the houses were demolished around 1960. Lintfieldbank had a miners' welfare institute (still standing, but now a community hall) which opened in the 1930s and provided a venue for the villagers and families from nearby houses and farms to meet socially. The welfare institute committee organised and held an annual gala day complete with queen and retinue. There are traces of a lint mill (see insert) which was last used in the 1930s as a joiner's shop or furniture factory. Although the houses have gone, families with former connections with Lintfieldbank still return to the hall for WRI meetings, carpet bowls and other events. Birkhill, the oldest house in the district (built in the late 1600s) stands near to Lintfieldbank. Just a little further along the road is Cairnhouse, where several houses were demolished in the 1940s for the road widening of the A74 Glasgow to Carlisle Road. The name Cairnhouse was derived from a cairn that once stood in the area, although there is now no trace of it.

Although about 800 feet above sea level, Coalburn has many arable farms, mainly along the course of the Poniel Burn and in valleys of the River Nethan and Logan Water. The principal landowner to the south was the Greenshields family of Westoun House, which had some cottages on their grounds including Westerhouse, above. In the early 1980s the family sold their estate to Scottish Coal, which developed Dalquhandy (pronounced Dewhannie), the largest opencast working of coal in Europe. Two features of the land have been preserved. The first is the huge outcrop of rocks called Wallace's Caves. The second is the private burial ground of the Greenshields family, with five headstones listing several generations of the family, several of whom died abroad in tea plantations where they made their fortune. The photograph shows Mrs Ross with William, Christine and Jenny Knowles in 1913. Jenny, who became Mrs McLaren, still lives in Coalburn and told me that her parents reared ten children in two rooms in part of the double cottage on the left. In Jenny's early years the building on the right with the outside stone stairs was called 'the granary', as foodstuffs for Westoun House were kept there. The favourite walk for generations of Coalburn villagers was 'ower the mair' and 'back by Westoun', but access stopped at the start of the opencast workings in 1988.

The school at Douglas Water initially took pupils from the ages of five to fourteen, but later became a primary before closing in the late 1990s when a new primary school was built at Rigside. Drew's sweet shop was in the small row of houses on the immediate left of the school. Some of the miners' rows can be seen in the background, with the railway bridge over the main road to the right. On the same road as the school and to its right is Anstruther Place, part of which included the shops of the Douglas Water Co-operative Society.

The co-operative store supplied villagers with most of their needs. Bill Davidson told me how as a boy in the 1930s he would be sent for the 'messages', and would queue with other customers to be served. One commodity asked for constantly was paraffin oil for lamps and stoves. The oil was kept in a large tank at the back of the store. To save time and effort, the junior apprentice who filled the cans at the tank would come into the shop and bawl out 'Ony mair ile cans?'. Bill continued: 'I can remember my astonishment when modern technology was introduced at the store. The central cash desk was in the grocery department and it was connected to the bake shop, the butcher's and the drapery by a system of wires and pulleys which carried little cups for transferring sales slips and cash (or co-op tokens) to and from the cash desk. The cups were fired along the system by giving a spring-loaded handle a powerful yank. The system was later replaced by an arrangement of tubes using suction or air pressure to move cash containers between the departments.' As at the co-operatives in Coalburn and Douglas, members were assigned a number and a book which was placed in a box at the grocery counter. The co-ops paid a quarterly dividend on purchases, which needless to say was eagerly looked forward to by housewives in the less affluent days of the 1930s.

Ponfeigh Station, Douglas Water.

Even after the arrival of bus services in Lanarkshire in the 1920s, the railway remained the principal method of transport for inhabitants of Douglas Water. The station for the village (called Ponfeigh), was right in the centre, so very conveniently located. The line ran from Muirkirk to Inches, Douglas West, Happendon, Ponfeigh, Sandilands, and finally to Lanark, the terminus. There was a spur at Douglas Water to the colliery, where wagons were loaded every working day. Older residents will recall how important passenger trains were for getting to and from Lanark – for children taking courses at Lanark Academy, and for those going to work – especially the girls employed in the factories and shops.

Douglas Water was a 'dry' village, as the owner of the land in and around it wouldn't allow the opening of licensed premises. Men seeking a refreshment could walk to the Star Inn near Lesmahagow, or make their way to Douglas. As Bill Davidson told me: 'The five o'clock train on a Saturday was packed with men heading for the pubs and with folk of all ages going to the pictures at the Regal Cinema at Lanark. The return journey in the late trains after the men had enjoyed the convivial hospitality of the Lanark pubs was boisterous, and the noise of the singing of the inebriated could be heard all along the train when it stopped at Sandilands and at Ponfeigh. It was not unknown for the station 'barra' to be pressed into service to convey someone home who had temporarily lost the power of his legs.' All this was to end in October 1964 when passenger train services were withdrawn.

The village of Douglas Water is in Carmichael Parish, and census returns reveal a tremendous swell in the parish population, which rose from 593 in the year 1891 to 1,198 in 1901. This great increase was due to the Coltness Iron Company opening Douglas Colliery at Douglas Water in 1896, along with hastily erected rows to house the incoming miners and their families. (There is often confusion at the fact that Douglas Colliery was in Douglas Water and not in the village of Douglas.) By 1910, Douglas Colliery was employing 559 men – 480 underground and 79 above ground. 352 of the employed men were living in houses owned by the colliery at Douglas Water, with the others coming from Lanark, Douglas and Rigside. The smaller photograph shows Powell Street, with the United Free Church Hall at its head (now used by the Masonic Lodge Hozier 912). The larger photograph shows the back of the rows in Powell Street.

A photograph from the 1930s, when neighbours joined in to help wash the blankets. As well as the washtub on its stand and clothes basket, there is a wringer (obscured) on the left, which one of the women is leaning her elbow on. None of the women would ever have imagined that washdays would become so much easier when automatic washing machines and clothes dryers came into vogue. For that matter many housewives would never have imagined that in many homes blankets on beds would be replaced with duvets. Everyone recognises that coal miners faced danger underground every day at work, and that their toil was arduous and the surroundings uncongenial. Statistics show that each year *circa* 1900, a coal miner in Britain was killed every six hours,. For every one killed, 200 suffered some form of injury. For the wives and mothers of coal miners work in the home, although safe, was constant drudgery, and the working day often lasted eighteen hours. The housewives were renowned for their cheerfulness, however, as this photograph illustrates.

*Back row:* Mrs Johnstone; Peggy Welsh; Mrs Begg; Mrs Nellies.
*Middle row:* Mrs Downie; Mrs Welsh; Mrs Hamilton; Mrs Davidson; Mrs Hamilton.
*Children:* John Downie; David Crawford; David Downie.

Douglas Colliery was sunk in the Lanarkshire coalfield at Douglas Water by the Coltness Iron Company of Newmains after trial leases were secured from the Earl of Home in 1893. Although coal had been produced at Ponfeigh and Rigside for very many decades, the operations had never been on a large scale. Protracted negotiations had been necessary before the company's plans were approved by the Earl, who was anxious to preserve the amenities of the district. It is sad that these provisions did not prevent the area around Douglas Water being left disfigured when coal extraction by deep mining stopped in the 1960s. The photograph shows Douglas Colliery, which was unique in the respect that the stumpy chimney was not the usual height for dispersing smoke and fumes into the upper air. This was because the Earl didn't want it to be visible from his castle at Douglas. Coal extracted at Douglas Water was of excellent quality and was in great demand for engines pulling high-speed trains. It is in the local folklore that Douglas Water coal stoked the fires of the engine which pulled the Royal Train. This high-quality coal resulted in a period of steady employment in Douglas Water for over sixty years until the seams for deep-mining ran out, hastened by a raging and uncontrollable fire which broke out in a main seam.

The rows of houses at Newtonfoot were located at Douglas Colliery, and accommodated employees such as engineers, blacksmiths and joiners who needed to be available for repairs to breakdowns at the pit. The rows were demolished after the end of the Second World War.

Douglas Water Pipe Band heading a Masonic procession in the 1950s with the rows of Powell Street in the background. The building between the rows and the band was the slaughterhouse for local butchers. The band was in existence for around fifty years but ceased functioning when families moved away after the demolition of the rows. Featured in the front row (left to right) are Willie Mason (with stick); Willie Morris; Richard Haddow; Robert Fulton; Archie Templeton and Willie Wilkinson. Others in the band are Tom Kerr, Tarry Gold, Jean Hannah, Guy Whitefield, John Morris and Willie Fulton.

Douglas Water also had a silver band, subsidised at first by the Coltness Iron Company who owned the colliery. After it won the Championship (First Class) of Scotland in 1920 it went by the prestigious name of Douglas Colliery Prize Silver Band. The band competed and won prizes in subsequent years but folded soon after its last appearance in the Scottish Championships in 1955. The photograph shows the silver band leading the procession for the May Queen along Carmichael Street in the 1930s.

Rigside grew up as a mining community along a stretch of the A70, the road which runs from Edinburgh to Ayr. This was constructed as a turnpike road and a house (now demolished) for collecting tolls stood at Moorfoot. Moorfoot toll house also served as an inn, as was the custom with most toll houses, and a story – probably apocryphal but now embedded in local folklore – circulates about an incident that happened there. A coach arrived one evening at Moorfoot and two men entered the inn for refreshment. It was noticed that one man remained sitting motionless in the coach. The innkeeper, possibly touting for more business, asked the two men if the man in the coach would like a refreshment. The reply was 'I don't think he would be interested'. It later transpired that the two men were the infamous body snatchers, Burke and Hare. The third man had been one of their murder victims and his propped-up corpse was being transported to Edinburgh to sell for medical research.